# TABLE OF CONTENTS

**Cooking & Baking Terms, Measurements & Abbreviations**
The Benton Kitchen
©Copyright 2012 by Nancy L Benton

## DISCLAIMER AND TERMS OF USE AGREEMENT:

**(Please Read This Before Using This Book)**

This information is for educational and informational purposes only. The content is not intended to be a substitute for any professional advice, diagnosis, or treatment.

The authors and publisher of this book and the accompanying materials have used their best efforts in preparing this book.

The authors and publisher make no representation or warranties with respect to the accuracy, applicability, fitness, or completeness of the contents of this book. The information contained in this book is strictly for educational purposes. Therefore, if you wish to apply ideas contained in this book, you are taking full responsibility for your actions.

The authors and publisher disclaim any warranties (express or implied), merchantability, or fitness for any particular purpose. The author and publisher shall in no event be held liable to any party for any direct, indirect, punitive, special, incidental or other consequential damages arising directly or indirectly from any use of this material, which is provided "as is", and without warranties. As always, the advice of a competent legal, tax, accounting, medical or other professional should be sought where applicable.

The authors and publisher do not warrant the performance, effectiveness or applicability of any sites listed or linked to in this book. All links are for information purposes only and are not warranted for content, accuracy or any other implied or explicit purpose. No part of this may be copied, or changed in any format, or used in any way other than what is outlined within this course under any circumstances. Violators will be prosecuted.

This book is © Copyrighted by ePubWealth.com.

## Introduction – Learn it and then apply it!

Hello again, and welcome to my 6<sup>th</sup> ebook dealing with something that is very important – Cooking & Baking Terms, Measurements & Abbreviations.

These subjects are important and cannot be glossed over if it is your desire to become a good cook and baker.

My mother actually sat me down and made me study the material outlined in this book and would ask me questions as we cooked together…and God help me if I answered wrong!

My mother was never one for incompetency; she believed the adage that a person should NEVER do their best but they should DO what is required.

I need you to embrace this philosophy too. Doing your best just gives you an excuse to fail; doing what is required guarantees your success!

Cooking and Baking are the spice of life; they are important because they bring contentment and quality of life to individuals. They also provide a "family experience" where the entire family can participate and take part in the joys of cooking and baking.

In today's world, anything that brings families together in active participation is important and let's face it; everybody loves to eat and cooking crosses national boundaries too.

I sincerely hope you enjoy this book and keep it close so that you can use it to make correct measurements and understandings of the terms and abbreviations.

Happy Cooking & Baking…Nancy L. Benton

## Chapter 1 – Most Common Cooking and Baking Terms

There are many "common" terms used in recipes for different cooking or mixing methods. Here is a list of some of the most common ones that are used most often that you may come across when baking and an explanation of what they mean to help you with your baking techniques:

| | |
|---|---|
| **Boil** | To cook until liquid is so hot it forms bubbles |
| **Broil** | To cook directly under a heating element |
| **Chill** | To place in the refrigerator to lower a food's temperature |
| **Chop** | To cut into pieces with a sharp knife or chopper |
| **Combine** | To mix ingredients together |
| **Cream** | To beat until smooth, soft and fluffy |
| **Cube** | To cut into 1/4-inch cubes |
| **Cut** | To mix a solid fat into a flour mixture with a pastry blender, a fork or two knives |
| **Dice** | To cut food into 1/8-inch cubes |
| **Dot** | Drop bits of butter or cheese here and there over food |
| **Drain** | To pour off liquid |

| | |
|---|---|
| **Flour** | To coat greased pans or dishes with a fine coat of flour. Shake out extra flour |
| **Fold** | To mix gently by bringing rubber scraper down through mixture, across the bottom, up and over top until blended |
| **Fry** | To cook in hot fat |
| **Garnish** | To decorate a finished dish with colorful food to make it look pretty |
| **Grate** | Rub against a grater to cut into small shreds |
| **Grease** | To spread the bottom and/or sides of a pan with shortening to prevent sticking |
| **Grill** | To cook directly over a heating element or hot coals |
| **Knead** | To fold, turn, and press dough with heel of your hand in order to develop the gluten and make dough more elastic |
| **Ladle** | To dip and serve liquid with a ladle |
| **Melt** | To heat until it liquefies |
| **Mince** | To chop or cut into tiny pieces |
| **Mix** | To stir foods together |
| **Panfry** | To cook in fat in a skillet |

| | |
|---|---|
| **Pare** | To cut off the outside skin, as from an apple or potato |
| **Peel** | To pull off the outer skin, as from a banana or an orange |
| **Pit** | To take out the seeds |
| **Roll** | Flatten and spread with a rolling pin |
| **Sauté** | To cook in small amount of fat in a skillet |
| **Scald** | To heat milk just below a boiling point. Tiny bubbles will form around the edge |
| **Shred** | To cut into very thin strips |
| **Sift** | To put dry ingredients like flour through a sifter or sieve |
| **Simmer** | To cook in liquid over low heat so bubbles form slowly |
| **Stir** | To mix round and round with a spoon |
| **Toss** | To mix lightly |
| **Well** | A hole made in dry ingredients in which you pour liquid |
| **Whip** | To beat with a rotary egg beater or electric mixer to add air |

## Chapter 2 – An Extensive Glossary of Cooking & Baking Terms

**All-Purpose Flour** — This is a wheat flour that is made from the milling of hard wheat or a mixture of hard and soft wheat. It can be bleached or not and is often enriched with iron and the vitamins folic acid, riboflavin, folic acid, niacin. All-purpose flour is commonly used in homes for noodles, cookies, cakes, quick breads, pastries, and certain yeast breads.

**Amaranth Flour** — Amaranth flour is milled from amaranth seeds, and since it lacks gluten, it can only be used in yeast breads if it is combined with a wheat flour. Many people enjoy this flour due to its strong flavor that is particularly well suited for savory pastries or breads. It also gives quick breads a smooth texture.

**Ascorbic Acid** — More commonly known as vitamin C, ascorbic acid is added to bread flour because it enables bread dough to gain a greater volume when it is baked into a loaf.

**Baking** — Baking is the process of using dry heat to cook food. It is usually performed in an oven.

**Baking Pan** — A baking pan is a pan of any shape or size that is used to bake cookies, pies, breads, biscuits, cakes, or specialty baked goods. Today, they are usually made of light- to heavy-gauge steel, although heavy-gauge aluminum is used in the construction of two-layer, insulated baking pans. Mid-gauge aluminum is most often used for the pans that test kitchens rely upon to define baking standards such as time and temperature. *See also definitions for cookie pan, nonstick, baking sheet, jelly-roll pan, and insulated pan.*

**Baking Powder** — Baking powder is a product used for leavening that is a combination of baking soda and either citric or tartaric acid or a mixture of the two. This powder, when it is wet and hot, will react without acid from other ingredients in the food that is baked. Home-use baking powder typically has two kinds of acid, one that reacts to liquids in the baking dough and the other reacts when baking heats the product. The baked goods are made lighter via the carbon dioxide that is produced by the powder. Over time, baking powder can lose its strength, and it should be tested if it has been sitting on the shelf for a while. Good baking powder will bubble strongly when one teaspoon of it is mixed with one-quarter cup of hot water.

**Baking Sheet** — A baking sheet is a rigid metal sheet, often with one or more turned-up edges, that can be used to bake biscuits, breads, cookies, and other goods. There are several types of baking sheets. Dark, heavy-gauge baking pans are used to bake specialty goods with crisp crusts. Test kitchens will use shiny, heavy-gauge aluminum to bake and brown evenly. Soft-cookies, rolls, and tender-crusted breads are often baked using insulated sheets, which are two sheets of aluminum with a space for air in between them. *See also cookie sheet, jelly-roll pan, and insulated bakeware.*

**Baking Soda** — Baking soda reacts with an acid when it is wet to produce carbon dioxide and lighten baked

11

goods. The wet, acidic ingredients that typically cause this reaction with baking soda in a batter include buttermilk, sour milk, citrus juices, chocolate, vinegar, or honey, and the reaction will begin immediately when liquids are added to the dry ingredients. Baking soda is a bicarbonate of soda that is created from trona, a mineral that is mined in Green River, Wyoming.

**Baking Stone** — A baking stone is a plate of stone or other unglazed, tile-like material. It can be round or rectangular, and it is used to help simulate the properties of a brick oven floor in a home oven. Place the stone on the lowest rack in the oven and only preheat the stone if the manufacturer recommends it. The food that is to be baked can be placed directly on the stone or in a pan and then on a stone.

**Barley Flour** — Barley flour has a sweet taste and it gives cakes, quick breads, and cookies moisture and a light texture. It is milled from hulled barley and it is low in gluten.

**Beating** — Beating is the process of stirring or whipping with a spoon, electric mixture, wire whisk, or beater to create a smooth mixture of ingredients.

**Blend** — To blend ingredients is to mix two or more of them together with a spoon or whisk or an appliance such as a blender, mixer, or processor.

**Bloom** 1.) In bread, bloom is the brown color found in the crust of a well-baked loaf. .

2.) In chocolate, bloom refers to pale, grayish streaks or blotches that appear on the surface of chocolate that demonstrates that separation of cocoa butter from the chocolate itself. It occurs when chocolate has been stored in an environment that is too warm, but it does not mean that the chocolate is no longer usable.

**Bran** — Bran is the name of the outer layers of a grain kernel that are found just below the hull of the grain. Dietary fiber and other nutrients can be added to cereals and baked goods with bran, which makes up approximately 14.5 percent of all types of whole-wheat flour. The bran that results when bran layers are removed from a grain kernel during milling is known as "miller's bran."

**Bread Flour** — Bread flour is the preferred flour for those who use bread machines to bake bread. It is an unbleached wheat flour that is high in protein, which aids in the development of better yeast bread. It is good to use a bread flour that is enriched with various vitamins and minerals.

**Brownie** — This favorite desert is a chewy, dense, cake-like cookie that is sliced into bars for serving. Usually, brownies are chocolate-flavored and colored brown, hence their name.

**Buckwheat Flour** — Despite its name, buckwheat is not a relative of the grain known as wheat. Buckwheat is originally from Russia, and its distinctive flavor is treasured in pancakes and other baked goods like multi-grain breads. Appropriately, Russian blini made from buckwheat flour, as are groats and kasha. Buckwheat flour has not gluten and it is created from the grinding of hulled buckwheat seeds.

**Bulgur** — Bulgur refers to whole-wheat kernels after they have been steamed, dried, and cracked. Bulgur can be ground up and made into flour, or it can be soaked or cooked for addition to baked goods.

**Butter** — According to U.S. standards, butter is comprised of 80 percent milk fat and 20 percent milk solids and water. It is created through churning cream into a semi-solid, and it can be salted or unsalted. Bakers use butter on account of its flavor and its facility for creating crispness, flaky layers, flavors, tenderness, and a golden-brown color.

**Cake Flour** — Cake flour is a low-protein flour that is silky and fine in texture that can be used for pastries, cakes, cookies, and certain breads.

**Canning & Pickling Salt** — This is a salt that can be used just like table salt in baking. It is a pure, granulated salt that has no free-flowing agents or other additives, and it may cake if it is exposed in an environment that has a greater than 75 percent relative humidity. *See also salt.*

**Chocolate** — This favorite and familiar food and ingredient gets its name from xocolatl, an Aztec word that means "bitter water." Many forms of chocolate are used in baking, but whether it is unsweetened, milk, bittersweet, or semi-sweet chocolate, all of these forms use a base of "cocoa liquor" that is derived from ground, roasted, and blended small pieces of the cacao bean called nibs. *See also the other types of chocolate listed in this glossary.*

**Chop** — To chop is to cut up food into tiny bits.

**Cocoa Butter** — The portion of the cacao bean that is fat is known as cocoa butter.

**Cocoa Powder** — Fermented, roasted, dried, and cracked cacao beans can be made into an unsweetened powder called cacao powder. The nibs or small pieces of the cacao beans are ground up in order to make this powder, and 75 percent of the cacao butter is extracted to form the thick paste that is known as cocoa butter. Dutch cocoa is a special cocoa powder with a neutralized acidity due to its having been treated with alkali.

**Combine** — To combine ingredients is to mix them together.

**Confectioners'/Powdered Sugar** — One of the most widely used baking ingredients is confectioners' or powdered sugar, which is a granulated sugar crushed into a fine powder and combined with cornstarch. Only about 3 percent of the final product is cornstarch, which helps prevent the confectioners' sugar from clumping.

**Convection Cooking** — Convection cooking is a method used to cook certain foods faster, and it also allows the baker to cook a larger quantity of food and use multiple baking racks all at the same time. In convection cooking, a fan will circulate heated air continually in the oven, and the thoroughness of the cooking means that convection cooking often requires lower oven temperatures.

**Convection Oven** — The convection oven has a fan to circulate hot air around that which is being cooked on a continual basis, allowing the baking of several products on different racks all at once. A convection oven can be either gas or electric, may not need preheating, and the temperature required to cook a product in a conventional oven can often be reduced by 25 degrees in a convection oven.

**Cookie** — Deriving its name from the Dutch word koekje or "little cake," a cookie is a sweet, hand-held small cake with a flour base.

**Cookie Pan** —Cookie pans are flat, rectangular pans made of rigid steel or aluminum. Its four sides will all have a lip of 5/8–3/4 inches high to keep the cookies from sliding off when it is moved. This lip also makes it easier to take the pan out of the oven. In many cases, the "cookie pans" used for home baking are actually jelly roll pans.

**Cookie Sheet** — Ranging in size from 10x8 inches to 20x15 inches, cookie sheets are flat, rectangular baking pans made of rigid aluminum or steel. Two of the four sides on a cookie sheet will have no raised edge in order to facilitate the removal of baked cookies.

**Cool** — To cool hot foods is to reduce their temperature until they are neither very hot nor very cold.

**Cooling Rack** — Baked goods are often cooled on a cooling rack, which is typically a rectangular grid made of thick wire with "feet" or "legs" to raise it off the countertop and allow cooler air to circulate all around the finished good. Usually, baked goods will be cooled for a short while on their pan before they are removed and put on a cooling rack. After they are done cooling on this rack, they can be placed in storage or frozen. The exceptions to this rule are yeast breads, which are usually transferred from a baking pan immediately to a cooling rack in order to keep the crust from getting soggy.

**Corn Bread** — Corn bread is a quick bread made from a flour incorporating 50 percent or more cornmeal. Corn bread can be thick and light or thin and crisp, and common forms of corn bread include Johnnycakes, spoon bread, and hushpuppies.

**Corn Flour** — Corn flour is flour that is made from the milling of whole corn. This flour has a corn flavor and is great in cornbread, waffles, and muffins, and when mixed with cornmeal.

**Cornmeal** — This is a medium, coarse, or fine meal made from dry degerminated or whole grain kernels of corn (yellow, blue, or white).

**Creaming** — Creaming is the process of mixing sugars and fats like butter, margarine, or shortening together with a mixer, large spoon, or beaters until the mixture is creamy in its appearance.

**Cut In** — To cut in is to use two knives or a pastry blender to combine cold fats (butter, margarine, or shortening) with flour or sugar without creaming or mixing air in the ingredients. A crumbly- or grainy-looking mixture is what results.

**Degerminated** — A degerminated food is a grain food that has had its germ removed in the process of milling.

**Dissolve** — To dissolve is to mix a dry substance into a liquid until the solids have all disappeared. For example, bakers can dissolve sugar into water, yeast into water, and more.

**Dry Ingredients** — Dry ingredients are those recipe ingredients that are dry and might need to be blended before they are added to another kind of mixture in the recipe. Dry ingredients can include sugar, salt, baking cocoa, spices, flour, and herbs.

**Dry Measuring Cups** — Some of the standard home-baking measuring tools used in the United States are dry measuring cups. These cups have straight sides with a handle attached to them at the top, and they come in graduated sizes including ¼ cup, 1/3 cup, ½ cup, 1, and 2 cup measurements. Usually they nest within one another for more storage. As one would expect from their name, dry ingredients like sugar, cornmeal, brown sugar, and flour are measured using these cups. These ingredients are spooned into the cup and then leveled off for measuring using a straight-edged knife or other utensil.

**Dust** — Dusting is the light sprinkling of a baked good or other surface with a dry ingredient like flour, meal, or powdered sugar.

**Eggs** — In baking, eggs can perform many tasks for a recipe, including thickening, binding, leavening, coating, glazing, moisturizing, drying, or emulsifying. They also introduce flavor, color, and nutrients into the baked good, or they can be used in frostings to slow crystallization. The standard-size egg called for in most recipes is large, unless the recipe says otherwise.

**Egg Wash** — An egg wash is a mixture that gives a rich color or gloss to the crust of a baked good when it is brushed on the unbaked surface o the product. It is made from combining one whole egg, egg white, or egg yolk with one tablespoon cold milk or water.

**Fermentation** — Fermentation is the chemical change in a food during the baking process in which enzymes leavens a dough and helps add flavor. In baking it is the first stage in which bread dough is allowed to rise before being shaped. Fermenting agents include yeast and other bacteria and microorganisms.

**Flour** — The major ingredient in the vast majority of baked goods, flour can be made from many different kinds of grains and other substances like beans, legumes, seeds, corn, oats, soybeans, teff, quinoa, amaranth, buckwheat, rye, spelt, and more. Wheat flours, however, are by far the most common flours used in baking.

**Focaccia** — Focaccia is an Italian bakers' snack whose name comes from the Latin term *focus* or hearth. Originally, focaccia was baked on a stone hearth.

**Gluten** — This protein is found in wheat and various cereal flours. Although some people are allergic to it, gluten makes up the structure of the bread dough and holds the carbon dioxide that is produced by the yeast or other substance during the fermentation process. When flour is combined with liquids, gluten develops as the liquid and flour is mixed and then kneaded. Formed from the proteins glutenin and gliadin, gluten provides the elasticity and extensibility or stretch for bread dough.

**Gluten-Free** — Some people are allergic to gluten, but there are many ways to bake without producing the gluten protein. Gluten-free flours include rice, corn, soy, amaranth, and potato flours. Stone-ground, graham, or whole-wheat flours made from hard or soft wheats or both kinds are also usable. These are produced through the milling of whole-wheat kernels or combining white flour, bran and germ. Even though these gluten-flours may differ in coarseness from their gluten counterparts, the nutritional value is virtually the same.

**High-Altitude Baking** — Baking in environments at higher elevations require adjustments in ingredients and temperatures to produce the same results as baking that occurs in lower altitudes. When cooking is done at an elevation greater than 3,000 feet, amounts of liquids, leaving agents, and sugar, as well as oven temperature may need to be changed.

**Honey** — Produced from flower nectar through the work of bees, honey is an all-natural sweetener that produces a golden-colored curst and holds moisture in different baked goods. Its color and flavor will vary according to the nectar that the bees use.

**Ice Cream Salt** — The coarse solar or rock salt used to help freeze ice cream should never be used in baking as it is not food grade. *See also salt.*

**Instant-Read Thermometer** — This is a stainless-steel probe thermometer that will register a temperature almost immediately when it is inserted into a mixture, dough, liquid or meat. Bakers typically use it in the baking of yeast breads.

**Insulated Bakeware** — Insulated bakeware is metal bakeware that is made up of two layers of metal with layer of air in between. Typically, insulated bakeware results in more consistent baking results than when it is done with its non-insulated counterpart. The bottom crust also tends to have less browning. When insulated bakeware is used, longer bake times may be needed for most baked goods, though the temperature will not need to be adjusted. Cakes and brownies made in such insulated pans, however, will require a temperature 25 degrees higher than that which the recipe lists.

**Invert Sugar** — Used in fondant icings for cakes, invert sugar is sugar syrup that has been slightly heated and exposed to small amount of acid in order to break up sucrose into fructose and glucose and reduce crystal size in the sugar.

**Jelly-Roll Pan** — Known commercially as a "half-sheet pan," a jelly-roll pan is a rectangular baking pan with a one inch edge and dimensions, usually, of 18x13 inches. Jelly-roll pans that are used for home baking come in a variety of sizes, and perhaps the most common one recommended in recipes is 15½x10½x1. Usually, a jelly-roll pan is used to bake sponge cakes, bars, or sheet cakes, and it derives its name from the fact that the sponge cake for a jelly-roll cake is baked in this kind of pan.

**Kneading** — Kneading is the process of working dough with the heels of one's hands, pressing and folding it and turning it a quarter of a turn after each time the dough is pressed and folded.

**Kosher Salt** — Kosher salt is used to top baked goods, kosher meat, or for recipes where coarse salt is preferred because it has a coarse-flake structure. Usually, kosher salt will not be iodized, but it may have an anti-caking agent included within it.

**Leavening** — Leavening refers to the production of a gas in a dough batter using an agent like baking powder, yeast, baking soda, or even eggs. Leavening agents work via the production of carbon dioxide in the dough, and long ago these agents were also known as "lifters."

**Liquid Measure** — A liquid measure is a clear, hard, plastic, or glass cup that can be used for pouring because of its special lip. Most of the time, a liquid measure is a quart or pint-sized tool that is marked with lines to help measure liquids in home-baking recipes. The lines will mark the levels in ounces, milliliters and sizes of 1/8, ¼, 1/3, ½, 2/3, ¾, 1 cup, and more. When baking at home, all liquids should be measured in this cup, and the cup should be placed on a flat surface for accuracy.

**Margarine** — Margarine, which may be salted or not, was created as an alternative to butter in the late nineteenth century. Eighty percent of margarine is partially-hydrogenated vegetable oil to give it a solid form and the other 20 percent is made up of flavoring, coloring, liquids, and other additives.

**Meal** — Grains or seeds that have been ground or milled more coarsely than normal flour make up meal.

**Measuring Cups and Spoons** — These are spoons and other containers of different, graduated sizes that can be used to measure liquid or dry ingredients accurately in the process of cooking and baking.

**Melt** — To melt is to heat an otherwise solid food until it achieves liquid form. In baking, sugar, butter, and chocolate are often melted.

**Milk Chocolate** — Milk chocolate is made up of a sweetened dark chocolate combined with other milk solids. At least 10 percent of the product will be chocolate liquor, and the milk solids will comprise at least 12 percent of the final product.

**Millet Flour** — Produced from whole millet, millet flour is a low-gluten, starchy flour that is finely ground. Its texture is quite similar to that of rice flour.

**Mixing** — Mixing is the art of combining two or more individual ingredients until no one ingredient can be seen or identified. This is usually accomplished through stirring with a spoon.

**Muffin Pans** — Muffin pans are used for the baking of muffins, and they come in several different sizes and shapes. There are even pans for "muffin tops." The muffin pan that is most commonly called for has 6 or 12 muffin cups that measure 2½ inches in diameter at the top, although there are also mini-muffin tins in 12- and 24-cup sizes. These mini-muffins are also known as "tea muffins," and whether the muffins being baked are large or small, lining the tins with paper liners or greasing the muffin cups will produce the best results. *See also insulated pans, nonstick, and baking pans.*

**No-Knead** — Also known as "batter breads," no-knead is a baking method for yeast breads that can be produced without any kneading.

**Nonstick** — Nonstick coating is a coating applied to a pan to prevent baked goods from sticking to it. It can be applied via high-temperature coil-coating before the pan is actually formed, or it can be sprayed onto the pan after it has been constructed. Nonstick coatings are usually silicone-based or PTFE-based (polytetraflourethylene or Teflon).

**Nut Flour** — Nut flour is made up on nut meats that have been finely ground. The nuts that are used can be either toasted or not, and the flour is used for breads, cookies, cakes, and pastry crusts.

**Nuts** — Nuts are the dry fruits of legumes, seeds, or trees. Made up of an edible kernel surrounded by a dry, hard shell, nuts are high in nutrients and flavor. They can have as much as 90 percent fat, although nut fats are primarily monounsaturated and very healthy. The different textures and flavors of nuts can provide much sensory satisfaction in baked goods.

**Oats** — Oats are made up of any grain that is hulled, cleaned, toasted, and cooked whole (groats). These groats can also be steel-cut, steamed, or rolled (flattened). Rolled oats can be made quick-cooking when they receive additional cuts, and they can be used interchangeably with other oats in baking because they are whole grains. Instant oats, however, have been more finely cut and cooked, so they cannot be used in place of normal oats.

**Oat Flour** — Oat flour is made up of rolled oats or groats that have been finely ground.

**Oat Bran** — Oat bran refers to the outer layers of an oat kernel. Oat bran is a good additive for baked goods as it is high in soluble fiber.

**Oils** — Liquid fats that are derived from pressing plants and their seeds/nuts are known as oils. This oil can be extracted via cold-pressing or solvent extraction, and common home-baking oils include, safflower, corn, canola, olive, sunflower, and soybean oils. None of these plant oils have cholesterol, but they all vary in the amount of poly-unsaturated, mono-unsaturated, and saturated fats they contain.

**Oven** — An enclosed space with parts that supply air flow and heat in order to cook. Electric elements or gas burners are used in conventional ovens for baking, broiling, or roasting, while convection ovens also include a fan to circulate heated air all around the food. Electric ovens usually have controls to cycle the temperatures of the upper and lower elements for consistent cooking temperatures. Some ovens are clean by hand (standard oven), while others are self-cleaning or continuous cleaning. Ovens can range in width from 20 to 36 inches, and they can exist as drop-ins, slide-ins, free-standing, or wall-mounted appliances. In recent years, ovens that use microwaves or halogen lights to increase cooking speed have been developed.

**Pastry Flour** —Pastry flour is low in gluten and high in starch. It is usually fine-textured and soft, and it comes in bleached, unbleached, and whole wheat varieties. Soft red or white wheat is typically used in the production of pastry flours.

**Preheat** — To preheat an oven is to heat an empty oven to the proper temperature for the recipe before the food product is placed within it.

**Proof** — Proof is the amount of time that a baking product is allowed to rise after it has been shaped and placed in or on the proper pan. Generally speaking, most baked goods proof until they have doubled in size or until a lightly placed finger on the good leaves a marked indentation. A humid, draft-free location with a temperature of between 95 and 100 degrees is required for proofing, and at home a slightly damp, clean, non-terry cloth towel or plastic wrap that has been sprayed with a pan spray can be laid on the product in order to retain moisture and keep the crust from drying out. Many ovens have a proofing feature, so consult the instructions before baking.

**Pumpernickel** — Pumpernickel is a rye flour of medium-to-course grinding that is light brown in its color. Sometimes it is called "medium rye," which is mixture of wheat and rye flours to produce the bread. Often, molasses will be added to the dough to improve color and flavor in the pumpernickel bread.

**Punch Down** — This term used in reference to bread dough describes the point at which a dough has doubled in its size or when a marked dent is visible after two fingers are lightly pressed into the dough about half of an inch. Punching down a dough can be achieved via touching the dough with the fingers, making a fist, and pushing it down into the center of the dough before pulling the dough edges into the center and turning the dough over. After doing this, cover the dough and let it rest or rise again before it is shaped into a loaf.

**Quick Bread** — Quick bread is a bread that can be made very quickly because not time is needed for kneading or rising in its production.

**Quinoa Flour** — Quinoa flour made from the grinding of quinoa grain. It is free of gluten and very nutritious. Its tender, moist crumb is favored for waffles, fruitcakes, pancakes, and cookies.

**Red Wheat** — The second major kind of U.S. wheat, red wheat refers to three of the six classes of wheat recognized in the United States. Its kernels have a reddish color, and it is ground into flour for baking.

**Rye Flour** — Rye flour is milled from the rye grain and is low in gluten. It is also darker and heavier than wheat flour, and is sold in dark, medium, and light forms for use in baking at home. Light and medium rye flour has had most of its bran removed, while dark rye flour is a whole grain flour. *See also pumpernickel.*

**Salt** — Used to add flavor to baked goods and/or control fermentation in breads, salt, also known as sodium chloride (NaCl), salt is made one of three different ways. Salt (Sodium Chloride - NaCl) can be produced three ways. It can be made through the evaporation of salt brine in shallow ponds, the mining of deposits of rock salts, or by boiling and evaporating a brine of higher purity. Soft pretzels and other unique breads are often topped with coarse salt.

**Salt Substitute** — Used in order to reduce sodium intake, a salt substitute is usually granular potassium chloride. Since it has a bitter taste, it is not usually recommended for baking.

**Sauté** — To sauté is to cook or brown food in a small amount of hot fat or oil. This softens the food and releases its flavors.

**Scratch Baking** — Scratch baking begins with the use of basic ingredients like sugar, butter, leavening, and flour, and makes use of a recipe, not pre-made mixes.

**Sea Salt** — Sea salt is a salt produced via the evaporation outdoors of salt brine in shallow ponds. The amount of refining of sea salt will vary, as will its coarseness. Sea salt is suitable for baking unless it is very coarse.

**Self-Rising Cornmeal** — As one of the first convenience baking mixes, self-rising cornmeal has helped shorten the time it takes for people to make cornbreads and other cornmeal-based products. Most self-rising cornmeal is a blend of cornmeal (1½ cups), all-purpose flour (½ cup), baking powder (1 tablespoon), and salt (1 teaspoon).

**Self-Rising Flour** — Self-rising flour is another early "convenience mix" that when used in a recipe, allows for the baking powder and salt in the directions to be ignored. It is usually a combination of 1 cup all-purpose flour, 1½ teaspoons baking powder and ½ teaspoon salt.

**Semi-Sweet Chocolate** — Semi-sweet baking chocolate is a chocolate containing anywhere between 15 and 35 percent chocolate liquor plus sugar, cocoa butter, sugar, lecithin, and vanilla. Though it is not interchangeable with milk chocolate, it can be substituted for bittersweet or sweet chocolate in recipes that call for those forms of chocolate.

29

**Semolina Flour** — Also known as pasta flour, semolina flower is made through the grinding of semolina (granules) that come from durum wheat. Many specialty breads will include semolina or part-semolina flour in their ingredients.

**Spreads** — Spreads are solids or semi-solids in tubs or sticks containing less than 80 percent fat. They are not good for baking on account of their high water content.

**Soy Flour** — Hulled and roasted soybeans can be milled and ground to produce whole-grain, high-protein soy flour. This flour can be fat free, low fat or full fat depending on how it is produced.

**Sprinkle** — To sprinkle is to scatter small particles of toppings or sugars over a surface like cake, bread, frosting, and more.

**Standard** — Standards are recipes, methods, ingredients, measuring tools, and equipments that are used to produce consistent results in a particular product in home baking. Standards are a great help to both manufacturers and consumers.

**Staple** — A staple is one or more of the most important items, grown, sold, or made in a specific place, country, or region.

**Starter** — Starters are mixtures of sugar, water, yeast, and flour that are permitted to ferment in a warm location until they are foamy. These starters can be used in lieu of a package of yeast in breads, and usually a portion of two cups is the amount used. Usually this amount is taken after the mixture has been fed with more flour and water, something that needs to be done every two weeks after the starter has begun. In between feedings, the starter is often kept in a refrigerator.

**Stir** — To stir is to use a spoon to mix ingredients with a spoon using a figure-eight or circular motion.

**Stone-ground Flour or Meal** — This is a flour or meal that results from the grinding of grain between two stoners. It can be coarse or fine, though it is usually made up of whole grains.

**Sugar** — Though most people are not aware of this fact, sugar or sucrose occurs as a carbohydrate in every fruit and vegetable. It is the major product of photosynthesis, or the method by which plants convert energy from the sun into food. Most of the sugar used in home cooking is made in large quantities from sugar beets and sugar cane. There are several different kinds of sugar. *Granulated Sugar* is often called "white sugar" and is made up of fine or extra-fine white sugar crystals. *Brown Sugar* is made up of sugar crystals contained in a molasses-based syrup. Brown sugar comes in dark and light varieties according to the amount of molasses used, and the different forms can be substituted for one another according to taste. *Confectioners'* or *Powdered Sugar* has been defined earlier in this list. *Raw Sugar* contains about 98 percent sucrose and is tan or brown in its color. Although it is often found in foods, the USDA does not consider it fit for such uses. Raw sugar is coarse and made via the evaporation of clarified sugar cane juice. *Turbinado Sugar* is a sugar given a light tan color via its washing in a centrifuge. Its surface molasses is removed, making it closer to refined sugar than its raw counterpart.

**Table Salt** — Table salt, which is also known as granulated salt, is produced through the boiling and evaporation of brine. Table salt is often iodized, and anti-caking agents are usually added to it.

**Temperature** — This refers to the intensity of heat occurring in a baked product, mixture, or oven. In the United States, temperature is measured in degrees Fahrenheit, although the Celsius scale is used in much of the rest of the world.

**Texture** — The appearance and feel of a cut part of a cake or bread.

**Underproofed Loaves or Rolls** — These are rolls and breads that though they have been shaped, have not attained the volume or height that is desired before they are baked.

**Unleavened** — This term describes baked goods that do not use a leavening agent like baking soda, cream of tartar, baking powder, or yeast.

**Unbleached Flour** — An unbleached flour is one that has bleached naturally in its aging process without the addition of maturing agents. It is no different from bleached flour nutritionally, and it can be used interchangeably with its bleached counterpart in baking.

**Vegetable Shortening** — Vegetable shortening is a soybean or cottonseed oil that has been hydrogenated in order to make it a solid. Being 100 percent fat with no additives like water, milk fat, or other solids, it is almost flavorless and good for making baked goods flaky and tender.

**Wheat Flour** — Wheat flour is a popular flour used for cakes, waffles, pastries, and more when it milled from soft white or red wheat or for yeast breads, bagels, certain rolls, hearth breads, and pizza crust when milled from hard white or red wheat. Home baking wheat flours (or "family flours" according to the milling industry) can be unbleached or bleached all-purpose, pastry, whole-wheat, cake, graham, and bread flours. Some breads are made from high-protein durum wheat or semolina wheat flours, but such flours are usually reserved for pasta.

**Whip Beating** — Whip beating is the process of incorporating air into a food rapidly via a mixer, beater, or whip in order to increase its volume.

**White Chocolate** — While chocolate is a mixture of cocoa butter, lecithin, vanilla, milk solids and vanilla. True white chocolate always includes cocoa butter, and those products that do not contain it but are called white chocolate are actually more properly called confectionary or summer coating. White chocolate chips or pieces are popularly used in home baking.

**White Wheat** — U.S. wheat is classified into six different classes, three of which have a bran coat that is "white" or pale to amber in its color. Such white wheats include soft white wheat, durum wheat, and hard white wheat. *See also red wheat.*

**Whole Grain** — A whole grain food makes use of whole or ground kernels of grains like barley, corn, oat, wheat, and rye in its production.

**Whole-Wheat Flour** — Whole-wheat flour is made from the whole kernel of white or red wheat. Usually, whole-wheat flour is made in flour mills, but it can also be stone-ground in a mill. Another name for whole-wheat flour is graham flour.

## Chapter 3 – Advanced Glossary of Terms

Al dente
Italian for "to the tooth." It describes pasta that is cooked until it offers a slight resistance when bitten into, rather than cooked until soft.

Almond paste
A creamy mixture made of ground, blanched almonds and sugar that's often used as a filling in pastries, cakes, and confections. For best baking results, use an almond paste without syrup or liquid glucose.

Anchovy paste
A mixture of ground anchovies, vinegar, and seasonings. Anchovy paste is available in tubes in the canned fish or gourmet section of the supermarket.

Artificial sweeteners
A category of sugar substitutes that have no nutritional value. Because they have unique attributes, they should not be substituted for other sweeteners unless a recipe calls for them specifically.

Arugula
A brightly-colored salad green with a slightly bitter, peppery mustard flavor. It is also called rocket and resembles radish leaves.

Bake

To cook food, covered or uncovered, using the direct, dry heat of an oven. The term is usually used to describe the cooking of cakes, other desserts, casseroles, and breads.

Baking ammonia
A compound also known as hartshorn powder that was once used as a leavening agent. It's most often used in Scandinavian baking and is available at pharmacies and through mail order. Cream of tartar is an acceptable substitute, although cookies made with it are less crisp than those made with baking ammonia. If you use baking ammonia for baking, use caution when opening the oven door because irritating ammonia-like fumes may be produced.

Baking powder
A combination of dry acid, baking soda, and starch that has the ability to release carbon dioxide in two stages: when liquid ingredients are added and when the mixture is heated.

Baking soda
A chemical leavening agent that creates carbon dioxide and is used in conjunction with acidic ingredients, such as buttermilk, sour cream, brown sugar, or fruit juices, to create the bubbles that make the product rise.

Balsamic vinegar
Syrupy and slightly sweet, this dark-brown vinegar is made from the juice of the white Trebbiano grape. It gets its body, color, and sweetness from being aged in wooden barrels.

Basmati rice
An aromatic, long grain brown or white rice from India and California. Basmati rice is nutty and fluffy. Use as you would regular long grain rice.

Baste
To moisten foods during cooking or grilling with fats or seasoned liquids to add flavor and prevent drying. In general, recipes in this cookbook do not call for basting meat and poultry with pan juices or drippings. That's because basting tools, such as brushes and bulb basters, could be sources of bacteria if contaminated when dipped into uncooked or undercooked meat and poultry juices, then allowed to sit at room temperature and used later for basting.

Batter
An uncooked, wet mixture that can be spooned or poured, as with cakes, pancakes, and muffins. Batters usually contain flour, eggs, and milk as their base. Some thin batters are used to coat foods before deep frying.

Bean sauce, bean paste
Popular in Asian cooking, both products are made from fermented soybeans and have a salty bean flavor. Japanese bean paste is called miso.

Bean threads
Thin, almost transparent noodles made from mung bean flour. They also are called bean noodles or cellophane noodles.

Beat

To make a mixture smooth by briskly whipping or stirring it with a spoon, fork, wire whisk, rotary beater, or electric mixer.

Bias-slice
To slice a food crosswise at a 45-degree angle.

Blackened
A popular Cajun cooking method in which seasoned fish or other foods are cooked over high heat in a super-heated heavy skillet until charred, resulting in a crisp, spicy crust. At home, this is best done outdoors because of the large amount of smoke produced.

Blanch
To partially cook fruits, vegetables, or nuts in boiling water or steam to intensify and set color and flavor. This is an important step in preparing fruits and vegetables for freezing. Blanching also helps loosen skins from tomatoes, peaches, and almonds.

Blend
To combine two or more ingredients by hand, or with an electric mixer or blender, until smooth and uniform in texture, flavor, and color.

Boil
To cook food in liquid at a temperature that causes bubbles to form in the liquid and rise in a steady pattern, breaking at the surface. A rolling boil occurs when liquid is boiling so vigorously that the bubbles can't be stirred down.

Bouillon
A bouillon cube is a compressed cube of dehydrated beef, chicken, fish, or vegetable stock. Bouillon granules are small particles of the same substance, but they dissolve faster. Both can be reconstituted in hot liquid to substitute for stock or broth.

Bouquet garni
A bundle of fresh herbs usually thyme, parsley, and bay leaf used to add flavor to soups, stews, stocks, and poaching liquids. They are often tied inside two pieces of leek leaf or in a piece of cheesecloth.

Braise
To cook food slowly in a small amount of liquid in a tightly covered pan on the range top or in the oven. Braising is recommended for less-tender cuts of meat.

Breading
A coating of crumbs, sometimes seasoned, on meat, fish, poultry, and vegetables. Breading is often made with soft or dry bread crumbs.

Brie
A soft, creamy cheese with an edible white rind. Brie from France is considered to be the best in the world.

Brine
Heavily salted water used to pickle or cure vegetables, meats, fish, and seafood.

Broil

To cook food a measured distance below direct, dry heat. When broiling, position the broiler pan and its rack so that the surface of the food (not the rack) is the specified distance from the heat source. Use a ruler to measure this distance.

Broth
The strained clear liquid in which meat, poultry, or fish has been simmered with vegetables and herbs. It is similar to stock and can be used interchangeably with it. Reconstituted bouillon can also be used when broth is specified.

Brown
To cook a food in a skillet, broiler, or oven to add flavor and aroma and develop a rich, desirable color on the outside and moistness on the inside.

Butter
For rich flavor, butter is usually the fat of choice. For baking, butter is recommended rather than margarine for consistent results. Salted and unsalted butter can be used interchangeably in recipes; however, if you use unsalted butter, you may want to increase the amount of salt in a recipe.

Butterfly
To split food, such as shrimp or pork chops, through the middle without completely separating the halves. Opened flat, the split halves resemble a butterfly.

Candied

A food, usually a fruit, nut, or citrus peel, that has been cooked or dipped in sugar syrup.

Caramelize
To brown sugar, whether it is granulated sugar or the naturally occurring sugars in vegetables. Granulated sugar is cooked in a saucepan or skillet over low heat until melted and golden. Vegetables are cooked slowly over low heat in a small amount of fat until browned and smooth.

Capers
The buds of a spiny shrub that grows from Spain to China. Found next to the olives in the supermarket, capers have an assertive flavor that can best be described as the marriage of citrus and olive, plus an added tang that comes from the salt and vinegar of their packaging brine. While the smaller buds bring more flavor than the larger buds, both can be used interchangeably in recipes.

Carve
To cut or slice cooked meat, poultry, fish, or game into serving-size pieces.

Cheesecloth
A thin 100-percent-cotton cloth with either a fine or coarse weave. Cheesecloth is used in cooking to bundle up herbs, strain liquids, and wrap rolled meats. Look for it among cooking supplies in supermarkets and specialty cookware shops.

Chiffonade

In cooking, this French word, meaning "made of rags," refers to thin strips of fresh herbs or lettuce.

Chili oil
A fiery oil, flavored with chili peppers, that's used as a seasoning.

Chili paste
A condiment, available in mild or hot versions, that's made from chili peppers, vinegar, and seasonings.

Chill
To cool food to below room temperature in the refrigerator or over ice. When recipes call for chilling foods, it should be done in the refrigerator.

Chocolate
In general, six types of chocolate are available at the supermarket:
Milk chocolate is at least 10-percent pure chocolate with added cocoa butter, sugar, and milk solids.
Semisweet and bittersweet chocolate can be used interchangeably. They contain at least 35-percent pure chocolate with added cocoa butter and sugar.
Sweet chocolate is dark chocolate that contains at least 15-percent pure chocolate with extra cocoa butter and sugar.
Unsweetened chocolate is used for baking and cooking rather than snacking. This ingredient contains pure chocolate and cocoa butter with no sugar added.
Unsweetened cocoa powder is pure chocolate with most of the cocoa butter removed. Dutch-process or European-

style cocoa powder has been treated to neutralize acids, making it mellower in flavor.

White chocolate, which has a mild flavor, contains cocoa butter, sugar, and milk solids. Products such as white baking bars, white baking pieces, white candy coating, and white confectionery bars are sometimes confused with white chocolate. While they are often used interchangeably in recipes, they are not truly white chocolate because they do not contain cocoa butter.

Chop
To cut foods with a knife, cleaver, or food processor into smaller pieces.

Chorizo (chuh-REE-zoh)
A spicy pork sausage used in Mexican and Spanish cuisine. Spanish chorizo is made with smoked pork, and Mexican chorizo is made with fresh pork.

Chutney
A condiment often used in Indian cuisine that's made of chopped fruit (mango is a classic), vegetables, and spices enlivened by hot peppers, fresh ginger, or vinegar.

Clarified butter
Sometimes called drawn butter, clarified butter is best known as a dipping sauce for seafood. It is butter that has had the milk solids removed. Because clarified butter can be heated to high temperatures without burning, it's also used for quickly browning meats. To clarify butter, melt the butter over low heat in a heavy saucepan without stirring. Skim off foam, if necessary. You will see a clear, oily layer on top of a milky layer. Slowly pour the clear

liquid into a dish, leaving the milky layer in the pan. The clear liquid is the clarified butter; discard the milky liquid. Store clarified butter in the refrigerator up to 1 month.

Coat
To evenly cover food with crumbs, flour, or a batter. Often done to meat, fish, and poultry before cooking.

Coconut milk
A product made from water and coconut pulp that's often used in Southeast Asian and Indian cooking. Coconut milk is not the clear liquid in the center of the coconut, nor should it be confused with cream of coconut, a sweetened coconut concoction often used to make mixed drinks such as piña coladas.

Cooking oil
Liquids at room temperature made from vegetables, nuts, or seeds. Common types for general cooking include corn, soybean, canola, sunflower, safflower, peanut, and olive. For baking, cooking oils cannot be used interchangeably with solid fats because they do not hold air when beaten.

Couscous (KOOS-koos)
A granular pasta popular in North Africa that's made from semolina. Look for it in the rice and pasta section of supermarkets.

Cream
To beat a fat, such as butter or shortening either alone or with sugar, to a light, fluffy consistency. May be done by

hand with a wooden spoon or with an electric mixer. This process incorporates air into the fat so baked products have a lighter texture and a better volume.

Crème fraîche
A dairy product made from whipping cream and a bacterial culture, which causes the whipping cream to thicken and develop a sharp, tangy flavor. If you can't find crème fraîche in your supermarket, you can make a substitute by combining 1/2 cup whipping cream (do not use ultra-pasteurized cream) and 1/2 cup dairy sour cream. Cover the mixture and let it stand at room temperature for two to five hours or until it thickens. Cover and refrigerate for up to one week.

Crimp
To pinch or press pastry or dough together using your fingers, a fork, or another utensil. Usually done for a piecrust edge.

Crisp-tender
A term that describes the state of vegetables that have been cooked until just tender but still somewhat crunchy. At this stage, a fork can be inserted with a little pressure.

Crumbs
Fine particles of food that have been broken off a larger piece. Crumbs are often used as a coating, thickener, or binder, or as a crust in desserts. Recipes usually specify either soft or fine dry bread crumbs, which generally are not interchangeable.

Crush

To smash food into smaller pieces, generally using hands, a mortar and pestle, or a rolling pin. Crushing dried herbs releases their flavor and aroma.

Curdle
To cause semisolid pieces of coagulated protein to develop in a dairy product. This can occur when foods such as milk or sour cream are heated to too high a temperature or are combined with an acidic food, such as lemon juice or tomatoes.

Curry paste
A blend of herbs, spices, and fiery chilies that's often used in Indian and Thai cooking. Look for curry paste in Asian markets. Curry pastes are available in many varieties and are sometimes classified by color (green, red, or yellow), by heat (mild or hot), or by a particular style of curry (such as Panang or Masaman).

Cut in
To work a solid fat, such as shortening, butter, or margarine, into dry ingredients. This is usually done with a pastry blender, two knives in a crisscross fashion, your fingertips, or a food processor.

Dash
Refers to a small amount of seasoning that is added to food. It is generally between 1/16 and 1/8 teaspoon. The term is often used for liquid ingredients, such as bottled hot pepper sauce.

Deep-fry

To cook food by completely covering with hot fat. Deep-frying is usually done at 375 degrees.

Deglaze
Adding a liquid such as water, wine, or broth to a skillet that has been used to cook meat. After the meat has been removed, the liquid is poured into the pan to help loosen the browned bits and make a flavorful sauce.

Demi-glace (DEHM-ee-glahs)
A thick, intense meat-flavor gel that's often used as a foundation for soups and sauces. Demi-glace is available in gourmet shops or through mail-order catalogs.

Dip
To immerse food for a short time in a liquid or dry mixture to coat, cool, or moisten it.

Direct Grilling
Method of quickly cooking food by placing it on a grill rack directly over the heat source. A charcoal grill is often left uncovered, while a gas grill is generally covered.

Dissolve
To stir a solid food and a liquid food together to form a mixture in which none of the solid remains. In some cases, heat may be needed in order for the solid to dissolve.

Double boiler

A two-pan arrangement where one pan nests partway inside the other. The lower pot holds simmering water that gently cooks heat-sensitive food in the upper pot.

Drawn
A term referring to a whole fish, with or without scales, that has had its internal organs removed. The term "drawn butter" refers to clarified butter.

Dredge
To coat a food, either before or after cooking, with a dry ingredient, such as flour, cornmeal, or sugar.

Dressed
Fish or game that has had guts (viscera) removed. In the case of fish, gills are removed, the cavity is cleaned, and the head and fins remain intact. The scales may or may not be removed.

Drip pan
A metal or disposable foil pan placed under food to catch drippings when grilling. A drip pan can also be made from heavy-duty foil.

Drizzle
To randomly pour a liquid, such as powdered sugar icing, in a thin stream over food.

Dust
To lightly coat or sprinkle a food with a dry ingredient, such as flour or powdered sugar, either before or after cooking.

Egg roll skins
Pastry wrappers used to encase a savory filling and make egg rolls. Look for these products in the produce aisle of the supermarket or at Asian markets. Egg roll skins are similar to, but larger than, wonton skins.

Egg whites, dried
Pasteurized dried egg whites can be used where egg whites are needed; follow package directions for reconstituting them. Unlike raw egg whites, which must be thoroughly cooked before serving to kill harmful bacteria, pasteurized dried egg whites can be used in recipes that do not call for egg whites to be thoroughly cooked. Keep in mind that meringue powder may not be substituted, as it has added sugar and starch. Find dried egg whites in powdered form in the baking aisle of many supermarkets and through mail-order sources.

Eggs
Keep in mind that you should avoid eating foods that contain raw eggs. Eggs should be cooked until both the yolk and white are firm; scrambled eggs should not be runny. Cook casseroles and other dishes that contain eggs until they register 160 degrees F on a food thermometer. If you have a recipe that calls for the eggs to be raw or undercooked (such as Caesar salads and homemade ice cream), use shell eggs that are clearly labeled as having been pasteurized to destroy salmonella; these are available at some retailers. Or use a widely available pasteurized egg product. If you have a recipe that calls for egg whites to be raw or undercooked, use pasteurized dried egg whites or pasteurized refrigerated liquid egg whites.

49

For cake recipes, allow eggs to stand at room temperature for 30 minutes before using. If the cake recipe calls for separated eggs, separate them immediately after removing them from the refrigerator and use them within 30 minutes. For all other recipes, use eggs straight from the refrigerator.

Emulsify
To combine two liquid or semiliquid ingredients, such as oil and vinegar, that don't naturally dissolve into each other. One way to do this is to gradually add one ingredient to the other while whisking rapidly with a fork or wire whisk.

Extracts, oils
Products based on the aromatic essential oils of plant materials that are distilled by various means. In extracts, the highly concentrated oils are usually suspended in alcohol to make them easier to combine with other foods in cooking and baking. Almond, anise, lemon, mint, orange, peppermint, and vanilla are some commonly available extracts.

Some undiluted oils are also available, usually at pharmacies. These include oil of anise, oil of cinnamon, oil of cloves, oil of peppermint, and oil of wintergreen. Do not try to substitute oils for ground spices in recipes. Oils are so concentrated that they're measured in drops, not teaspoons. Oil of cinnamon, for example, is 50 times stronger than ground cinnamon. You can, however, substitute 1 or 2 drops of an oil for 1/2 teaspoon extract in frosting or candy recipes.

Fats, oils

See specific ingredients, such as butter, margarine, shortening, lard, or cooking oil.

Fava bean
A tan, flat bean that looks like a large lima bean. It is available dried, canned, and, occasionally, fresh.

Feta
A tangy, crumbly Greek cheese made of sheep's or goat's milk.

Fillet
A piece of meat or fish that has no bones. As a verb, fillet refers to the process of cutting meat or fish into fillets.

Fish Sauce
A pungent brown sauce made by fermenting fish, usually anchovies, in brine. It's often used in Southeast Asian cooking.

Flake
To gently break food into small, flat pieces.

Flavored oils
Commercially prepared oils flavored with herbs, spices, or other ingredients, including avocado, walnut, sesame, hazelnut, and almond. In addition to using them in recipes when called for, try brushing them over grilled vegetables or bread, or experiment with them in your favorite vinaigrette recipe.

Flavoring

An imitation extract made of chemical compounds. Unlike an extract or oil, a flavoring often does not contain any of the original food it resembles. Some common imitation flavorings available are banana, black walnut, brandy, cherry, chocolate, coconut, maple, pineapple, raspberry, rum, strawberry, and vanilla.

Flour
A milled food that can be made from many cereals, roots, and seeds, although wheat is the most popular. Store flour in an airtight container in a cool, dry place. All-purpose flour may be stored for up to 8 months. Bread flour, cake flour, gluten flour, whole wheat flour, and other whole grain flours may be stored up to 5 months. For longer storage, refrigerate or freeze the flour in a moisture- and vaporproof container. Bring chilled flour to room temperature before using in baking. Here are the types of flour most commonly used in cooking:

All-purpose flour: This flour is made from a blend of soft and hard wheat flours and, as its name implies, can be used for many purposes, including baking, thickening, and coating. All-purpose flour usually is sold pre-sifted and is available bleached or unbleached. Bleached flour has been made chemically whiter in appearance. Some cooks prefer the bleached flour to make their cakes and bread as white as possible, while other cooks prefer their flour to be processed as little as necessary. Both bleached and unbleached flour are suitable for home baking and can be used interchangeably.

Bread flour: This flour contains more gluten than all-purpose flour, making it ideal for baking breads, which rely on gluten for structure and height. If you use a bread machine, use bread flour instead of all-purpose flour for best results. Or use all-purpose flour and add 1 or 2 tablespoons of gluten flour (available in supermarkets or health food stores).

Cake flour: Made from a soft wheat, cake flour produces a tender, delicate crumb because the gluten is less elastic. It's too delicate for general baking, but to use it for cakes, sift it before measuring and use 1 cup plus 2 tablespoons of cake flour for every 1 cup all-purpose flour specified.

Gluten flour: Because whole-grain flours are low in gluten, some whole-grain bread recipes often call for a little gluten flour to help the finished loaf attain the proper texture. Sometimes called wheat gluten, gluten flour is made by removing most of the starch from high-protein, hard-wheat flour. If you can't find gluten flour at a supermarket, look for it at a health food store.

Pastry flour: A soft wheat blend with less starch than cake flour. It is used for making pastry.

Self-rising flour: An all-purpose flour with salt and a leavener, such as baking powder, added. It is generally not used for making yeast products.

Specialty flours: Specialty flours, such as whole wheat, graham, rye, oat, buckwheat, and soy, generally are combined with all-purpose flour in baking recipes because none has sufficient gluten to provide the right amount of elasticity on its own.

Flour (verb)

To coat or dust a food or utensil with flour. Food may be floured before cooking to add texture and improve browning. Baking utensils sometimes are floured to prevent sticking.

Flute
To make a decorative impression in food, usually a piecrust.

Fold
A method of gently mixing ingredients without decreasing their volume. To fold, use a rubber spatula to cut down vertically through the mixture from the back of the bowl. Move the spatula across the bottom of the bowl, and bring it back up the other side, carrying some of the mixture from the bottom up over the surface. Repeat these steps, rotating the bowl one-fourth of a turn each time you complete the process.

Food coloring
Liquid, paste, or powdered edible dyes used to tint foods.

French
To cut meat away from the end of a rib or chop to expose the bone, as with a lamb rib roast.

Frost
To apply a cooked or uncooked topping, which is soft enough to spread but stiff enough to hold its shape, to cakes, cupcakes, or cookies.

Fry

To cook food in a hot cooking oil or fat, usually until a crisp brown crust forms. To panfry is to cook food, which may have a very light breading or coating, in a skillet in a small amount of hot fat or oil. To deep-fat fry (or French fry) is to cook a food until it is crisp in enough hot fat or oil to cover the food. To shallow fry is to cook a food, usually breaded or coated with batter, in about an inch of hot fat or oil. To oven fry is to cook food in a hot oven, using a small amount of fat to produce a healthier product.

Garlic
The strongly scented, pungent bulb of a plant related to an onion. A garlic clove is one of the several small segments that make up a garlic bulb. Elephant garlic is larger, milder, and more closely related to the leek. Store firm, fresh, plump garlic bulbs in a cool, dry, dark place; leave bulbs whole because individual cloves dry out quickly. Convenient substitutes are available; for each clove called for in a recipe use either 1/8 teaspoon garlic powder or 1/2 teaspoon bottled minced garlic.

Garnish
To add visual appeal to a finished dish.

Gelatin
A dry ingredient made from natural animal protein that can thicken or set a liquid. Gelatin is available in unflavored and flavored forms. When using, make sure the gelatin powder is completely dissolved.
To dissolve one envelope of unflavored gelatin: Place gelatin in a small saucepan and stir in at least 1/4 cup water, broth, or fruit juice. Let it stand 5 minutes to

soften, then stir it over low heat until the gelatin is dissolved.

Do not mix gelatin with figs, fresh pineapple (canned pineapple is not a problem), fresh ginger, guava, kiwifruit, and papaya, as these foods contain an enzyme that prevents gelatin from setting up.

Some recipes call for gelatin at various stages of gelling. "Partially set" means the mixture looks like unbeaten egg whites. At this point, solid ingredients may be added. "Almost firm" describes gelatin that is sticky to the touch. It can be layered at this stage. "Firm" gelatin holds a cut edge and is ready to be served.

Giblets

The edible internal organs of poultry, including the liver, heart, and gizzard. (Although sometimes packaged with the giblets, the neck is not part of the giblets.) Giblets are sometimes used to make gravy.

Ginger

The root of a semitropical plant that adds a spicy-sweet flavor to recipes (also called gingerroot). Ginger should be peeled before using. To peel, cut off one end of the root and use a vegetable peeler to remove the brown outer layer in strips. To grate ginger, use the fine holes of a grater. To mince ginger, slice peeled ginger with the grain (lengthwise) into thin sticks. Stack the sticks in a bundle and cut them finely. Ginger stays fresh two or three weeks in the refrigerator when wrapped loosely in a paper towel. For longer storage, place unpeeled ginger in a freezer bag and store in freezer. Ginger will keep indefinitely when frozen, and you can grate or slice the ginger while it's frozen. In a pinch, ground ginger can be used for grated fresh ginger. For 1 teaspoon grated fresh ginger, use 1/4 teaspoon ground ginger.

Ginger, crystallized
A confection made from pieces of ginger (gingerroot) cooked in a sugar syrup, then coated with sugar. Also known as candied ginger. Store in a cool, dry, dark place.

Glacé (gla-SAY)
The French term for "glazed" or "frozen." In the United States, it describes a candied food.

Glaze
A thin, glossy coating. Savory glazes are made with reduced sauces or gelatin; sweet glazes can be made with melted jelly or chocolate.

Gluten
An elastic protein present in flour, especially wheat flour, that provides most of the structure of baked products.

Grate
To rub food, such as hard cheeses, vegetables, or whole nutmeg or ginger, across a grating surface to make very fine pieces. A food processor also may be used.

Grease
To coat a utensil, such as a baking pan or skillet, with a thin layer of fat or oil. A pastry brush works well to grease pans. Also refers to fat released from meat and poultry during cooking.

Grind

To mechanically cut a food into smaller pieces, usually with a food grinder or a food processor.

## Gumbo
The word gumbo is from an African word meaning "okra." This Creole stew contains okra, tomatoes, and onions as well as various meats or shellfish such as shrimp, chicken, or sausage. It is thickened with a roux.

## Half-and-half
A mixture of equal parts cream and milk. It has about 12 percent milk fat and cannot be whipped.

## Haricot vert
French for "green string bean", these beans are particularly thin and tender.

## Heavy cream
Also called heavy whipping cream. Heavy cream contains at least 46 percent milk fat and is the richest cream available. It can be whipped to twice its volume.

## Hoisin Sauce
A sauce, popular in Asian cooking, that brings a multitude of sweet and spicy flavors to a dish: fermented soybeans, molasses, vinegar, mustard, sesame seeds, garlic, and chiles. Look for hoisin sauce alongside the soy sauce in most supermarkets or in Asian markets.

## Hominy
Dried white or yellow corn kernels that have been soaked in lime or lye to remove the hull and germ. It is available canned or dried. Ground hominy is used to make grits.

Honey

A sweet, sticky sweetener that's produced by bees from floral nectar. Honey is now available in more than 300 varieties in the United States. Its flavor depends on the flowers from which the honey is derived; most honey is made from clover, but other sources include lavender, thyme, orange blossom, apple, cherry, buckwheat, and tupelo. Generally, the lighter the color, the milder the flavor. Store honey at room temperature in a dark place. If it crystallizes (becomes solid), reliquefy it by warming the honey jar slightly in the microwave oven or in a pan of very hot tap water. If the honey smells or tastes strange, toss it out.

Note that honey should not be given to children who are younger than one year old because it can contain trace amounts of botulism spores. These spores could trigger a potentially fatal reaction in children with undeveloped immune systems.

Hors d'oeuvre (or-DERV)

French term for small, hot or cold portions of savory food served as an appetizer.

Ice

To drizzle or spread baked goods with a thin frosting.

Indirect grilling

Method of slowly cooking food in a covered grill over a spot where there are no coals. Usually the food is placed on the rack over a drip pan, with coals arranged around the pan.

## Jelly roll
Dessert made by spreading a filling on a sponge cake and rolling it up into a log shape. When other foods are shaped "jelly-roll-style," it refers to rolling them into a log shape with fillings inside.

## Juice
The natural liquid extracted from fruits, vegetables, meats, and poultry. Also refers to the process of extracting juice from foods.

## Knead
To work dough with the heels of your hands in a pressing and folding motion until it becomes smooth and elastic. This is an essential step in developing the gluten in many yeast breads.

## Kosher salt
A coarse salt with no additives that many cooks prefer for its light, flaky texture and clean taste. It also has a lower sodium content than regular salt. Find it next to salt in the supermarket.

## Lard
A product made from pork fat that is sometimes used for baking. It's especially noted for producing light, flaky piecrusts. Today, shortening is commonly used instead of lard.

## Leavenings
Ingredients that are essential in helping batter and dough expand or rise during baking. If omitted, the baked products will be heavy and tough. See specific

ingredients, such as yeast, baking powder, and baking soda, for more information.

## Lemongrass
A highly aromatic, lemon-flavored herb often used in Asian cooking. To use, trim the fibrous ends and slice what remains into 3- to 4-inch sections. Cut each section in half lengthwise, exposing the layers. Rinse pieces under cold water to remove any grit and slice the lemongrass thinly. In a pinch, substitute 1/2 teaspoon finely shredded lemon peel for 1 tablespoon lemongrass.

## Light cream
Also called coffee or table cream. It usually contains about 20 percent milk fat and cannot be whipped.

## Marble
To gently swirl one food into another. Marbling is usually done with light and dark batters for cakes or cookies.

## Margarine
A product generally made from vegetable oil that was developed in the late 1800s as a substitute for butter. When baking, be sure to use a stick margarine that contains at least 80 percent fat. Check the nutritional information. It should have 100 calories per tablespoon.

## Marinade
A seasoned liquid in which meat, poultry, fish, shellfish, or vegetables are soaked to flavor and sometimes tenderize them. Most marinades contain an acid, such as wine or vinegar.

Marinate

To soak food in a marinade. When marinating foods, do not use a metal container, as it can react with acidic ingredients to give foods an off flavor. Always marinate foods in the refrigerator, never on the kitchen counter. To reduce cleanup, use a plastic bag set in a bowl or dish to hold the food you are marinating. Discard leftover marinade that has come in contact with raw meat. Or if it's to be used on cooked meat, bring leftover marinade to a rolling boil before using to destroy any bacteria that may be present.

Marsala

A fortified wine that can be either dry or sweet. Sweet Marsala is used both for drinking and cooking. Dry Marsala makes a nice pre-dinner drink.

Mash

To press or beat a food to remove lumps and make a smooth mixture. This can be done with a fork, potato masher, food mill, food ricer, or electric mixer.

Measure

To determine the quantity or size of a food or utensil.

Melt

To heat a solid food, such as chocolate, margarine, or butter, over very low heat until it becomes liquid or semi-liquid.

Milk and milk products

Varieties include:

Buttermilk: Buttermilk is a low-fat or fat-free milk to which a bacterial culture has been added. It has a mildly acidic taste. Sour milk, made from milk and lemon juice or vinegar, can be substituted in baking recipes.

Evaporated milk: Made from whole milk, canned evaporated milk has had about half of its water removed; it lends a creamy richness to many recipes, including pumpkin pie. Measure it straight from the can for recipes calling for evaporated milk; to use it in place of fresh milk, dilute it as directed on the can (usually with an equal amount of water) to make the quantity called for in the recipe. Evaporated milk is also available in low-fat and fat-free versions. Evaporated milk is not interchangeable with sweetened condensed milk.

Fat-free half-and-half: Made mostly from skim milk, with carrageenan for body, this product can bring a creamy flavor to recipes without added fat. Experiment using it in cornstarch or flour-thickened soup, sauce, and gravy recipes that call for regular half-and-half.

Light cream and half-and-half: Light cream contains 18 to 30 percent milk fat. Half-and-half is a mixture of milk and cream. They're interchangeable in most recipes; however, neither contains enough fat to be whipped.

Nonfat dry milk powder: When reconstituted, this milk product can be used in cooking.

Sour cream and yogurt: Sour cream is traditionally made from light cream with a bacterial culture added, while yogurt is made from milk with a bacterial culture added. Both are available in low-fat and fat-free varieties.

Sweetened condensed milk: This product is made with whole milk that has had water removed and sugar added. It is also available in low-fat and fat-free versions. Sweetened condensed milk is not interchangeable with evaporated milk or fresh milk.

Whipping cream: It contains at least 30 percent milk fat and can be beaten into whipped cream.

Whole, low-fat or light, reduced-fat, and fat-free milk: Because these milk types differ only in the amount of fat they contain and in the richness of flavor they lend to foods, they may be used interchangeably in cooking. Recipes in this cookbook were tested using reduced-fat (2 percent) milk.

Mince
To chop food into very fine pieces, as with minced garlic.

Mix
To stir or beat two or more foods together until they are thoroughly combined. May be done with an electric mixer, a rotary beater, or by hand with a wooden spoon.

Moisten
To add enough liquid to a dry ingredient or mixture to make it damp but not runny.

Mortar and pestle

A set that includes a bowl-shape vessel (the mortar) to hold ingredients to be crushed by a club-shape utensil (the pestle).

Mull
To slowly heat a beverage, such as cider, with spices and sugar.

Mushrooms, dried
Dried mushrooms swell into tender, flavorful morsels. Simply cover them in warm water and soak them for about 30 minutes. Rinse well and squeeze out the moisture. Remove and discard tough stems. Cook them in recipes as you would fresh mushrooms. Popular choices include oyster, wood ear, and shiitake.

Mushrooms, fresh
A plant in the fungus family, mushrooms come in many colors and shapes, with flavors ranging from mild and nutty to meaty, woodsy, and wild.

Nonstick cooking spray
This convenient product reduces the mess associated with greasing pans; it can also help cut down on fat in cooking. Use the spray only on unheated baking pans or skillets because it can burn or smoke if sprayed onto a hot surface. For safety, hold pans over a sink or garbage can when spraying to avoid making the floor or counter slippery.

Nuts
Dried seeds or fruits with edible kernels surrounded by a hard shell or rind. Nuts are available in many forms, such

as chopped, slivered, and halved. Use the form called for in the recipe. In most recipes, the nuts are selected for their particular flavor and appearance; however, in general, walnuts may be substituted for pecans, and almonds for hazelnuts, and vice versa.

When grinding nuts, take extra care not to overgrind them, or you may end up with a nut butter. If you're using a blender or processor to grind them, add 1 tablespoon of the sugar or flour from the recipe for each cup of nuts to help absorb some of the oil. Use a quick start-and-stop motion for better control over the fineness. For best results, grind the nuts in small batches and be sure to let the nuts cool after toasting and before grinding.

Pan-broil
To cook a food, especially meat, in a skillet without added fat, removing any fat as it accumulates.

Parbroil
To boil a food, such as vegetables, until it is partially cooked

Parchment paper
A grease- and heat-resistant paper used to line baking pans, to wrap foods in packets for baking, or to make disposable pastry bags.

Pare
To cut off the skin or outer covering of a fruit or vegetable, using a small knife or a vegetable peeler.

Parsnip

A white root vegetable that resembles a carrot. Parsnips have a mild, sweet flour and can be cooked like potatoes.

Pectin
A natural substance found in some fruits that makes fruit-and-sugar mixtures used in jelly- or jam-making set up. Commercial pectin is also available.

Peel
The skin or outer covering of a vegetable or fruit (also called the rind). Peel also refers to the process of removing this covering.

Pesto
Traditionally an uncooked sauce made from crushed garlic, basil, and nuts blended with Parmesan cheese and olive oil. Today's pestos may call on other herbs or greens and may be homemade or purchased. Tomato pesto is also available. Pesto adds a heady freshness to many recipes.

Phyllo dough (FEE-loh)
Prominent in Greek, Turkish, and Near Eastern dishes, phyllo consists of tissue-thin sheets of dough that, when layered and baked, results in a delicate, flaky pastry. The word phyllo (sometimes spelled filo) is Greek for "leaf." Although phyllo can be made at home, a frozen commercial product is available and much handier to use. Allow frozen phyllo dough to thaw while it is still wrapped; once unwrapped, sheets of phyllo dough quickly dry out and become unusable. To preserve sheets of phyllo, keep the stack covered with plastic wrap while

you prepare your recipe. Rewrap any remaining sheets and return them to the freezer.

Pinch
A small amount of a dry ingredient (the amount that can be pinched between a finger and the thumb).

Pine nuts
A high-fat nut that comes from certain varieties of pine trees. Their flavor ranges from mild and sweet to pungent. They go rancid quickly; store in the refrigerator or freezer. In a pinch, substitute chopped almonds or, in cream sauces, walnuts.

Pipe
To force a semisoft food, such as whipped cream or frosting, through a pastry bag to decorate food.

Pit
To remove the seed from fruit.

Plump
To allow a food, such as raisins, to soak in a liquid, which generally increases its volume.

Poach
To cook a food by partially or completely submerging it in a simmering liquid.

Pound
To strike a food with a heavy utensil to crush it. Or, in the case of meat or poultry, to break up connective tissue in order to tenderize or flatten it.

Precook
To partially or completely cook a food before using it in a recipe.

Preheat
To heat an oven or a utensil to a specific temperature before using it.

Process
To preserve food at home by canning, or to prepare food in a food processor.

Proof
To allow a yeast dough to rise before baking. Also a term that indicates the amount of alcohol in a distilled liquor.

Prosciutto
Ham that has been seasoned, salt-cured, and air-dried (not smoked). Pressing the meat gives it a firm, dense texture. Parma ham from Italy is considered to be the best.

Provolone
A southern Italian cheese made from cow's milk. Provolone is firm and creamy with a mild, smoky flavor. Because it melts so well, it is an excellent cooking cheese.

Puff pastry
A butter-rich, multilayered pastry. When baked, the butter produces steam between the layers, causing the dough to puff up into many flaky layers. Because warm, softened puff pastry dough becomes sticky and

unmanageable, roll out one sheet of dough at a time, keeping what you're not using wrapped tightly in plastic wrap in the refrigerator.

Puree
To process or mash a food until it is as smooth as possible. This can be done using a blender, food processor, sieve, or food mill; also refers to the resulting mixture.

Reconstitute
To bring a concentrated or condensed food, such as frozen fruit juice, to its original strength by adding water.

Reduce
To decrease the volume of a liquid by boiling it rapidly to cause evaporation. As the liquid evaporates, it thickens and intensifies in flavor. The resulting richly flavored liquid, called a reduction, can be used as a sauce or as the base of a sauce. When reducing liquids, use the pan size specified in the recipe, as the surface area of the pan affects how quickly the liquid will evaporate.

Rice
To force food that has been cooked through a perforated utensil known as a ricer, giving the food a somewhat ricelike shape.

Rice noodles
Thin noodles, popular in Asian cooking, that are made from finely ground rice and water. When fried, they puff into light, crisp strands. They can also be soaked to use in stir-fries and soups. Thicker varieties are called rice sticks. Find in Asian markets; substitute vermicelli or

capellini for thin rice noodles, linguine or fettuccine for thicker rice sticks.

### Rice papers
These round, flat, edible papers, made from the pith of a rice-paper plant, are used for wrapping spring rolls.

### Rice vinegar
A mild-flavored vinegar made from fermented rice. Rice vinegar is interchangeable with rice wine vinegar, which is made from fermented rice wine. Seasoned rice vinegar, with added sugar and salt, can be used in recipes calling for rice vinegar, though you may wish to adjust the seasonings. If you can't find rice vinegar, substitute white vinegar or white wine vinegar.

### Rind
The skin or outer coating, usually rather thick, of a food.

### Roast, roasting
A large piece of meat or poultry that's usually cooked by roasting. Roasting refers to a dry-heat cooking method used to cook foods, uncovered, in an oven. Tender pieces of meat work best for roasting.

### Roll, roll out
To form a food into a shape. Dough, for instance, can be rolled into ropes or balls. The phrase "roll out" refers to mechanically flattening a food, usually a dough or pastry, with a rolling pin.

### Roux (roo)

A French term that refers to a mixture of flour and a fat cooked to a golden- or rich-brown color and used for a thickening in sauces, soups, and gumbos.

Salsa
A sauce usually made from finely chopped tomatoes, onions, chilies, and cilantro. It is often used in Mexican and Southwestern cuisine.

Sauté
From the French word sauter, meaning "to jump." Sauteed food is cooked and stirred in a small amount of fat over fairly high heat in an open, shallow pan. Food cut into uniform size sautés the best.

Scald
To heat a liquid, often milk, to a temperature just below the boiling point, when tiny bubbles just begin to appear around the edge of the liquid.

Score
To cut narrow slits, often in a diamond pattern, through the outer surface of a food to decorate it, tenderize it, help it absorb flavor, or allow fat to drain as it cooks.

Scrape
To use a sharp or blunt instrument to rub the outer coating from a food, such as carrots.

Sea salt
This variety of salt is derived from the evaporation of sea water. Some cooks prefer it over table salt for its clean, salty flavor.

Sear

To brown a food, usually meat, quickly on all sides using high heat. This helps seal in the juices and may be done in the oven, under a broiler, or on top of the range.

Section

To separate and remove the membrane of segments of citrus fruits. To section oranges, use a paring knife to remove the peel and white rind. Working over a bowl to catch the juice, cut between one orange section and the membrane, slicing to the center of the fruit. Turn the knife and slide it up the other side of the section along the membrane, cutting outward. Repeat with remaining sections.

Sherry

A fortified wine that ranges from dry to sweet, and light to dark. Sherry can be enjoyed as a predinner or after-dinner drink, and it is also used in cooking.

Shortening

A vegetable oil that has been processed into solid form. Shortening commonly is used for baking or frying. Plain and butter-flavor types can be used interchangeably. Store in a cool, dry place. Once opened, use within 6 months. Discard if it has an odor or appears discolored.

Shred

To push food across a shredding surface to make long, narrow strips. Finely shred means to make long thin strips. A food processor also may be used. Lettuce and cabbage may be shredded by thinly slicing them.

Shrimp paste
A pungent seasoning made from dried, salted shrimp that's been pounded into a paste. Shrimp paste gives Southeast Asian dishes an authentic, rich flavor. The salty shrimp taste mellows during cooking. In a pinch, substitute anchovy paste, though it's not as boldly flavored.

Shuck
To remove the shells from seafood, such as oysters and clams, or the husks from corn.

Sieve
To separate liquids from solids, usually using a sieve.

Sift
To put one or more dry ingredients, especially flour or powdered sugar, through a sifter or sieve to remove lumps and incorporate air.

Simmer
To cook food in a liquid that is kept just below the boiling point; a liquid is simmering when a few bubbles form slowly and burst just before reaching the surface.

Skewer
A long, narrow metal or wooden stick that can be inserted through pieces of meat or vegetables for grilling. If using bamboo or wooden skewers, soak them in cold water for 30 minutes before you thread them to prevent burning.

Skim

To remove a substance, such as fat or foam, from the surface of a liquid.

## Slice
A flat, usually thin, piece of food cut from a larger piece. Also the process of cutting flat, thin pieces

## Snip
To cut food, often fresh herbs or dried fruit, with kitchen shears or scissors into very small, uniform pieces using short, quick strokes.

## Soba noodles
Made from wheat and buckwheat flours, soba noodles are a favorite Japanese fast food. In a pinch, substitute a narrow whole wheat ribbon pasta, such as linguine.

## Somen noodles
Made from wheat flour, these dried Japanese noodles are very fine and most often white. In a pinch, substitute angel hair pasta.

## Sorbet
French for "sherbet." Sorbets are made from water, sugar, and fruit juice or puree, then churned when freezing. They are different from sherbets in that they don't contain milk.

## Soymilk
Made of the liquid pressed from ground soybeans, soymilk can be a good substitute for cow's milk for people who do not consume dairy products. Plain, unfortified soymilk offers high-quality proteins and B vitamins. Substituting soymilk for regular milk is

possible in some cases, though the flavor may be affected. Experiment to see what is acceptable to you.

Springform pan
A round pan with high sides and a removable bottom. The bottom is removed by releasing a spring that holds the sides tight around it. This makes it easy to remove food from the pan.

Steam
To cook a food in the vapor given off by boiling water.

Steep
To allow a food, such as tea, to stand in water that is just below the boiling point in order to extract flavor or color.

Stew
To cook food in liquid for a long time until tender, usually in a covered pot. The term also refers to a mixture prepared this way.

Stir
To mix ingredients with a spoon or other utensil to combine them, to prevent ingredients from sticking during cooking, or to cool them after cooking.

Stir-fry
A method of quickly cooking small pieces of food in a little hot oil in a wok or skillet over medium-high heat while stirring constantly.

Stock

The strained clear liquid in which meat, poultry, or fish has been simmered with vegetables or herbs. It is similar to broth but is richer and more concentrated. Stock and broth can be used interchangeably; reconstituted bouillon can also be substituted for stock.

Sugar
A sweetener that's primarily made from sugar beets or sugarcane. Sugar comes in a variety of forms:

Brown sugar: A mix of granulated sugar and molasses. Dark brown sugar has more molasses, and hence, more molasses flavor than light brown sugar (also known as golden brown sugar). Unless otherwise specified, recipes in this cookbook were tested using light brown sugar. In general, either can be used in recipes that call for brown sugar, unless one or the other is specified.

Tip: To help keep brown sugar soft, store it in a heavy plastic bag or a rustproof, airtight container and seal well. If it becomes hard, you can resoften it by emptying the hardened sugar into a rustproof container and placing a piece of soft bread in the container; the sugar will absorb the moisture and soften in a day or two. After the sugar has softened, remove the bread and keep the container tightly closed.

Coarse sugar: Often used for decorating baked goods, coarse sugar (sometimes called pearl sugar) has much larger grains than regular granulated sugar; look for it where cake-decorating supplies are sold.

Granulated sugar: This white, granular, crystalline sugar is what to use when a recipe calls for sugar without specifying a particular type. White sugar is most commonly available in a fine granulation, though superfine (also called ultrafine or castor sugar), a finer grind, is also available. Because superfine sugar dissolves readily, it's ideal for frostings, meringues, and drinks.

Powdered sugar: Also known as confectioner's sugar, this is granulated sugar that has been milled to a fine powder, then mixed with cornstarch to prevent lumping.
Sift powdered sugar before using.

Raw sugar: In the United States, true raw sugar is not sold to consumers. Products labeled and sold as raw sugar, such as Demerara sugar and turbinado sugar, have been refined in some way. Cleaned through a steaming process, turbinado sugar is a coarse sugar with a subtle molasses flavor. It is available in many health food stores.
Vanilla sugar: Infused with flavor from a dried vanilla bean, vanilla sugar tastes great stirred into coffee drinks and sprinkled over baked goods. To make vanilla sugar, fill a 1-quart jar with 4 cups sugar. Cut a vanilla bean in half lengthwise and insert both halves into sugar. Secure lid and store in a cool, dry place for several weeks before using. It will keep indefinitely.

Tahini
A flavoring agent, often used in Middle Eastern cooking, that's made from ground sesame seeds. Look for tahini in specialty food shops or Asian markets.

Tamari
A dark, thin sauce made from soybeans. Tamari is a slightly thicker, mellower cousin of soy sauce and is used to flavor Asian dishes. In a pinch, substitute soy sauce.

Tamarind paste
A thick, tart, brown Asian flavoring that comes from the fruit of a tamarind tree.

Thickeners
Food substances used to give a thicker consistency to sauces, gravies, puddings, and soups. Common thickeners include:

Flour and cornstarch: All-purpose flour and cornstarch are starches commonly used to thicken saucy mixtures. Cornstarch produces a more translucent mixture than flour and has twice the thickening power. Before adding one to a hot mixture, stir cold water into a small amount. You can also combine either flour or cornstarch with cold water in a screw-top jar and shake until thoroughly blended. It is critical that the starch-water mixture be free of lumps to prevent lumps in your sauce or gravy.

Quick-cooking tapioca: This is a good choice for foods that are going to be frozen because, unlike flour- and cornstarch-thickened mixtures, frozen tapioca mixtures retain their thickness when reheated.

Tip: When using tapioca as a thickener for crockery cooking and freezer-bound foods, you can avoid its characteristic lumpy texture by grinding the tapioca with a mortar and pestle before adding to the recipe.

Toast
The process of browning, crisping, or drying a food by exposing it to heat. Toasting coconut, nuts, and seeds helps develop their flavor. Also the process of exposing bread to heat so it becomes browner, crisper, and drier.

Tomatoes, dried
Sometimes referred to as sun-dried tomatoes, these shriveled-looking tomato pieces boast an intense flavor and chewy texture. They're available packed in olive oil or dry. Follow recipe directions for rehydrating dry tomatoes. If no directions are given, cover with boiling water, let stand about 10 minutes or until pliable, then drain well and pat dry. Snip pieces with scissors if necessary. Generally, dry and oil-packed tomatoes can be used interchangeably, though the dry tomatoes will need to be rehydrated, and the oil-packed will need to be drained and rinsed.

Tortilla
A small, thin, flat bread, popular in Mexican cooking, that is made from corn or wheat flour and usually is wrapped around a filling. To warm and soften flour tortillas, wrap a stack of 8 to 10 in foil and heat in a 350 degree F oven for 10 minutes.

Toss
To mix ingredients lightly by lifting and dropping them using two utensils.

Vanilla

A liquid extract made from the seed of an orchid. Imitation vanilla, an artificial flavoring, makes an inexpensive substitute for vanilla. They can be used interchangeably in our recipes.

Vermouth
White wine that has been fortified and flavored with herbs and spices. Dry vermouth is white and is used as a before-dinner drink or in nonsweet drinks, such as a martini. Sweet vermouth is reddish brown and can be drunk straight or used in sweet mixed drinks. Vermouth often is used as a cooking ingredient.

Vinegar
A sour liquid that is a byproduct of fermentation. Through fermentation the alcohol from grapes, grains, apples, and other sources is changed to acetic acid to create vinegar.

Wasabi
A Japanese horseradish condiment with a distinctive, pale lime-green color and a head-clearing heat (at least if used in significant amounts). Wasabi is available as a paste in a tube or as a fine powder in a small tin or bottle. It's often used to flavor fish.

Weeping
When liquid separates out of a solid food, such as jellies, custards, and meringues.

Whip

To beat a food lightly and rapidly using a wire whisk, rotary beater, or electric mixer in order to incorporate air into the mixture and increase its volume.

Wonton wrappers
Stuffed savory Asian pastries. The wrappers, paper-thin skins used to make wontons, can be found in the produce aisle or in Asian markets. Wonton wrappers are similar to, but smaller than, egg roll skins.

**XXX or XXXX Confectioners' Sugar**
The Xs on the package of confectioners' sugar indicates how finely it has been ground. Four X sugar is slightly finer than 3 x sugar, but the two different kinds can be used interchangeably in the same recipe. Whether or not sifting of the powdered sugar is required will be determined by the recipe's particular directions.

Yeast
A tiny, single-celled organism that feeds on the sugar in dough, creating carbon dioxide gas that makes dough rise. Three common forms of yeast are:
Active dry yeast: This is the most popular form; these tiny, dehydrated granules are mixed with flour or dissolved in warm water before they're used.
Bread-machine yeast: This highly active yeast was developed especially for use in doughs processed in bread machines.
Quick-rising active dry yeast (sometimes called fast-rising or instant yeast): This is a more active strain of yeast than active dry yeast, and it substantially cuts down on the time it takes for dough to rise. This yeast is usually mixed with the dry ingredients before the warm liquids

are added. The recipes in this book were tested using active dry yeast.

## Yield
Yield is the amount of a baked good that results from the combination of a given amount of different baking ingredients.

## Zest
The colored outer portion of citrus fruit peel. It is rich in fruit oils and often used as a seasoning. To remove the zest, scrape a grater or fruit zester across the peel; avoid the white membrane beneath the peel because it is bitter.

## Chapter 4 – Common Recipe Abbreviations

| Recipe Abbreviations |
| --- |
| t = tsp. = teaspoon |
| T = Tbs. = Tablespoon |
| fl = fluid |
| oz = ounce |
| pkg = package |
| pt = pint |
| qt = quart |
| gal = gallon |
| lb = pound |

## HELPFUL HINTS WITH ACCURATE RECIPE MEASUREMENT

Measure dry ingredients with measuring spoons and cups for accuracy:

Measure liquid ingredients with glass measuring cups for accuracy.

**Measuring spoons:** Fill the measuring spoon with dry ingredient and draw a straight edge knife or spatula over the surface, making the ingredient level.

**Measuring cups:** Fill the cup and level by drawing the straight edge of knife or spatula over the top. *Dry ingredients such as flour, should be packed lightly into the measuring cup* . Some recipes request flour to be sifted before being measured. Brown sugar is usually stated to pack firmly. Shortening and margarine or butter, if used in solid form should be packed firmly.

**Glass measure:** Place the glass measuring cup on a flat surface and look at the line level needed, pour liquid into the glass until it reaches the desired line to measure the exact amount.

## Chapter 5 – Useful Cooking Measures

| Miscellaneous Measurements | |
|---|---|
| **Measure** | **Equivalent** |
| 1 dash | 1/4 teaspoon or less |
| 1 pinch | 1/8 teaspoon or less |
| juice of 1 lemon | 2 to 3 tablespoons |
| juice of 1 orange | about 1/2 cup |

# Chapter 6 – Fluid Measures

| Fluid Measure | | | | | | | | |
|---|---|---|---|---|---|---|---|---|
| In the United States, liquid measurement is not only used for liquids such as water and milk, it is also used when measuring other ingredients such as flour, sugar, shortening, butter, and spices. | | | | | | | | |
| | tsp. | Tbs. | fluid oz. | gill | cup | pint | quart | gallon |
| tsp. | 1 | 1/3 | 1/6 | 1/24 | 1/48 | - | - | - |
| Tbs. | 3 | 1 | 1/2 | 1/8 | 1/16 | 1/32 | - | - |
| fluid oz. | 6 | 2 | 1 | 1/4 | 1/8 | 1/16 | 1/32 | - |
| gill | 24 | 8 | 4 | 1 | 1/2 | 1/4 | 1/8 | 1/32 |
| cup | 48 | 16 | 8 | 2 | 1 | 1/2 | 1/4 | 1/16 |
| pint | 96 | 32 | 16 | 4 | 2 | 1 | 1/2 | 1/8 |
| quart | 192 | 64 | 32 | 8 | 4 | 2 | 1 | 1/4 |
| gallon | 768 | 256 | 128 | 32 | 16 | 8 | 4 | 1 |
| firkin | 6912 | 2304 | 1152 | 288 | 144 | 72 | 36 | 9 |
| hogshead | 48384 | 16128 | 8064 | 2016 | 1008 | 504 | 252 | 63 |

## Chapter 7 – Dry Measures

| Dry Measure |
|---|
| Dry measurements are not typically used in US recipes; dry measurements are used mainly for measuring fresh produce (e.g. berries are sold by the quart, apples by the bushel, or peck). Do not confuse dry measure with liquid measure, because they are not the same. |

|  | pint | quart | gallon | peck | bushel | cubic feet |
|---|---|---|---|---|---|---|
| **pint** | 1 | 1/2 | 1/8 | 1/16 | 1/64 | 0.019445 |
| **quart** | 2 | 1 | 1/4 | 1/8 | 1/32 | 0.03889 |
| **gallon** | 8 | 4 | 1 | 1/2 | 1/8 | 0.15556 |
| **peck** | 16 | 8 | 2 | 1 | 1/4 | 0.31111 |
| **bushel** | 64 | 32 | 8 | 4 | 1 | 1.2445 |
| **cubic feet** | 51.428 | 25.714 | 6.4285 | 3.2143 | 0.80356 | 1 |

# Chapter 8 – Miscellaneous Measures

| Miscellaneous Measurements | |
| --- | --- |
| **Measure** | **Equivalent** |
| 1 dash | 1/4 teaspoon or less |
| 1 pinch | 1/8 teaspoon or less |
| juice of 1 lemon | 2 to 3 tablespoons |
| juice of 1 orange | about 1/2 cup |

## Chapter 9 – Equivalent Measures

| Equivalent Measurements | |
| --- | --- |
| **Dash** = less than 1/8 teaspoon | **4 quarts (liquid)** = 1 gallon |
| **3 tsp.** = 1 tbsp. | **8 quarts (solid)** = 1 peck |
| **1 cup** = 1/2 pint | **4 pecks** = 1 bushel |
| **2 cups** = 1 pint | **16 ounces** = 1 pound |
| **2 pints (4 cups)** = 1 quart | |

## Chapter 10 – Tablespoon Measures

| Tablespoon Measurements | |
|---|---|
| **4 tbsp.** = 1/4 cup | **12 tbsp.** = 3/4 cup |
| **5 tbsp. + 1 tsp.** = 1/3 cup | **14 tbsp.** = 7/8 cup |
| **8 tbsp.** = 1/2 cup | **16 tbsp.** = 1 cup |
| **10 tbsp. + 2 tsp.** = 2/3 cup | |

## Chapter 11 – Metric Volume Measures

| Volume Measurements | |
|---|---|
| **1 teaspoon** = 5 ml | **2/3 cup** = 160 ml |
| **1 tablespoon** = 15 ml | **3/4 cup** = 180 ml |
| **1/4 cup** = 60 ml | **1 cup** = 240 ml |
| **1/3 cup** = 80 ml | **1 quart** = (4 cups) 1 liter |
| **1/2 cup** = 120 ml | **1 gallon** = (4 quarts) 4 liters |

# Chapter 12 – Metric Weight Measures

| Weight Measurements | |
|---|---|
| **1/2 ounce** = 15 g | **8 ounces** = 225 g |
| **1 ounce** = 30 g | **12 ounces** = 340 g |
| **3 ounces** = 85 g | **16 ounces (1 pound)** = 455 g |
| **4 ounces** = 115 g | **2 pounds** = 1 kg |

## Chapter 13 – Common Abbreviations

**tsp.** = teaspoon

**tbsp.** = tablespoon

**pt.** = pint

**qt.** = quart

**oz.** = ounce or ounces

**lb.** = pound or pounds

**sq.** = square

**min.** = minute or minutes

**hr.** = hour or hours

**doz.** = dozen

**ml** = milliliter

**l** = liter

**g** = gram

**kg** = kilogram

# Chapter 14 – Temperature Conversions

| Fahrenheit Degrees | Celsius Degrees | Gas Mark | Oven Term |
|---|---|---|---|
| 200 | 100 | 1/8 | Very Low |
| 225 | 110 | 1/4 | Very Low |
| 250 | 120 | 1/2 | Very Low |
| 275 | 140 | 1 | Low |
| 300 | 150 | 2 | Low |
| 325 | 160 | 3 | Low |
| 350 | 180 | 4 | Moderate |
| 375 | 190 | 5 | Moderate |
| 400 | 200 | 6 | Moderate |
| 425 | 220 | 7 | High |
| 450 | 230 | 8 | High |
| 475 | 240 | 9 | High |
| 500 | 260 | 10 | Very High |

# Chapter 15 – Measuring Conversions

| Spoons | Milliliters | Cups | Milliliters |
|--------|-------------|--------|-------------|
| 1/8 tsp | 1ml | 1/8 cup | 30ml |
| 1/4 tsp | 1.25ml | 1/4 cup | 60ml |
| 1/2 tsp | 2.5ml | 1/3 cup | 80ml |
| 1 tsp | 5ml | 1/2 cup | 125ml |
| 2tsp | 10ml | 2/3 cup | 170ml |
| 3tsp | 15ml | 3/4 cup | 190ml |
| 1D | 10ml | 1 cup | 250ml |
| 1T | 15ml | 2 cups | 500ml |
| 2T | 30ml | 3 cups | 750ml |
| 3T | 45ml | 4 cups | 1 litre |
| 4T | 60ml | | |

# Chapter 16 – Cake Tin Conversions

| Inches | Millimeters | Centimeters |
|--------|-------------|-------------|
| 5in | 125mm | 12.5cm |
| 6in | 150mm | 15cm |
| 7in | 180mm | 18cm |
| 8in | 200mm | 20cm |
| 9in | 230mm | 23cm |
| 10in | 250mm | 25cm |
| 11in | 280mm | 28cm |
| 12in | 300mm | 30cm |

## Chapter 17 – Square Cake Tin to Round Cake Tin Conversions

| Square Tin | Round Tin |
|---|---|
| 13cm or 130mm (5 inch) | 15cm or 150mm (6 inch) |
| 12.5cm or 125mm (5inch) | 18cm or 180mm (7 inch) |
| 18cm or 180mm (7 inch) | 20cm or 200mm (8 inch) |
| 20cm or 200mm (8 inch) | 23cm or 230mm (9 inch) |
| 23cm or 230mm (9 inch) | 25cm or 250mm (11 inch) |
| 25.5cm or 255mm(10inch) | 28cm or 280mm (11 inch) |
| 28cm or 280mm (11inch) | 30cm or 300mm (12 inch) |

## Chapter 18 – Microwave Oven Conversions

Microwave recipes generally give terms based on a 700W to a 750W microwave oven.

The times below are given in minutes and seconds using 100% power.

| 1000W | 850W | 750W | 650W | 550W | 450W |
|-------|-------|-------|-------|-------|-------|
| 00:40 | 00:45 | 00:50 | 01:00 | 01:10 | 01:25 |
| 01:20 | 01:30 | 01:45 | 02:00 | 02:20 | 02:55 |
| 01:55 | 02:15 | 02:35 | 03:00 | 03:30 | 04:20 |
| 02:35 | 03:05 | 03:30 | 04:00 | 04:45 | 05:45 |
| 03:15 | 03:50 | 04:20 | 05:00 | 05:55 | 07:15 |
| 03:55 | 04:35 | 05:10 | 06:00 | 07:05 | 08:40 |
| 04:35 | 05:20 | 06:05 | 07:00 | 08:15 | 10:05 |
| 05:10 | 06:05 | 06:55 | 08:00 | 09:25 | 11:35 |
| 05:50 | 06:50 | 07:50 | 09:00 | 10:40 | 13:00 |
| 06:30 | 07:40 | 08:40 | 10:00 | 11:50 | 14:25 |
| 09:45 | 11:30 | 13:00 | 15:00 | 17:45 | 21:40 |
| 13:00 | 15:15 | 17:20 | 20:00 | 23:40 | 28:55 |

# Chapter 19 – Substituting Ingredients

| | |
|---|---|
| 15ml corn flour / maizena | 30ml cake flour |
| 250ml self raising flour | 250ml cake flour + 5ml baking powder |
| 5ml cream of tartar | 10ml lemon juice or vinegar |
| 230g butter | 220ml cooking oil |
| 250ml melted butter | 250ml cooking oil |
| 250ml sugar | 200ml golden syrup or honey |
| 250ml sour milk | 250ml milk + 20ml lemon juice or vinegar |
| 250ml yoghurt | 250ml buttermilk or sour cream |
| 15ml fresh herbs | 5ml dried herbs |
| 5ml dry mustard powder | 15ml prepared mustard |

## Chapter 20 – Common Ingredient Conversions

**Flour**

| | | |
|---|---|---|
| 1 cup (250ml) | = | 100g |
| 1 tablespoon (15ml) | = | 8g |

**Sugar**

| | | |
|---|---|---|
| 1 cup (250ml) | = | 200g |
| 1 tablespoon (15ml) | = | 15g |

**Icing Sugar**

| | | |
|---|---|---|
| 1 cup (250ml) | = | 100g |
| 1 tablespoon (15ml) | = | 8g |

**Butter & Margarine**

| | | |
|---|---|---|
| 1 cup (250ml) | = | 200g |
| 1 tablespoon (15ml) | = | 15g |

**Crumbs**

| | | |
|---|---|---|
| 1 cup (250ml) | = | 50g |
| 1 tablespoon (15ml) | = | 4g |

**Rice**

| | | |
|---|---|---|
| 1 cup (250ml) | = | 210g |
| 1 tablespoon (15ml) | = | 16g |

## I Have a Special Gift for My Readers

I appreciate my readers for without them I am just another author attempting to make a difference. If my book has made a favorable impression please leave me an honest review. Thank you in advance for you participation.

My readers and I have in common a passion for the written word as well as the desire to learn and grow from books.

My special offer to you is a massive ebook library that I have compiled over the years. It contains hundreds of fiction and non-fiction ebooks in Adobe Acrobat PDF format as well as the Greek classics and old literary classics too.

In fact, this library is so massive to completely download the entire library will require over 5 GBs open on your desktop.

Use the link below and scan all of the ebooks in the library. You can select the ebooks you want individually or download the entire library.

The link below does not expire after a given time period so you are free to return for more books rather than clog your desktop. And feel free to give the link to your friends who enjoy reading too.

I thank you for reading my book and hope if you are pleased that you will leave me an honest review so that I can improve my work and or write books that appeal to your interests.

Okay, here is the link…
http://tinyurl.com/special-readers-promo

PS: If you wish to reach me personally for any reason you may simply write to mailto:support@epubwealth.com.

I answer all of my emails so rest assured I will respond.

## Meet the Author

Nancy L Benton was born in Buffalo, New York and has been married for 37-years. She is a highly sought after cook (not chef) and delights in her culinary talents. She believes in good food, the best ingredients, and affordability. She states, "I grew up in an Italian family and my mother made sure I participated in all household duties especially cooking. Some of my fondest childhood memories take me back to those weekends where I made homemade bread and pasta with my mother and the smells that would come out of the kitchen and permeate the house." Food is an experience and one that needs to be maximized since we require food daily.

### Visit some of her websites

http://www.AddMeInNow.com
http://www.AppliedMindSciences.com
http://www.BookbuilderPLUS.com
http://www.BookJumping.com
http://www.EmailNations.com
http://www.EmbarrassingProblemsFix.com
http://www.ePubWealth.com
http://www.ForensicsNation.com
http://www.ForensicsNationStore.com
http://www.FreebiesNation.com
http://www.HealthFitnessWellnessNation.com
http://www.Neternatives.com
http://www.PrivacyNations.com
http://www.RetireWithoutMoney.org
http://www.SurvivalNations.com
http://www.TheBentonKitchen.com

http://www.Theolegions.org
http://www.VideoBookbuilder.com

**Some Other Books You May Enjoy From ePubWealth.com, LLC Library Catalog**

### EPW Library Catalog Online
http://www.epubwealth.com/wp-content/uploads/2013/07/Leland-benton-private-turbo.pdf

### EPW Library Catalog Download
http://www.filefactory.com/f/562ef3ea1a054f0a

CPSIA information can be obtained at www.ICGtesting.com
Printed in the USA
BVOW04s2228300414

352236BV00010B/110/P